the Light

OF CHRISTMAS

A FAMILY GUIDE FOR CELEBRATING
CHRISTMAS EVE & CHRISTMAS DAY

T5-CCU-339

The Light of Christmas

© 2015 by Outreach, Inc.

All rights reserved. No part of this book may be reproduced in any form or by any electronic or mechanical means, including storage and retrieval systems, photocopy, recording, scanning, or other, without permission in writing from the publisher, except by a reviewer who may quote brief passages in a review.

Published by Outreach, Inc., Colorado Springs, CO 80919
www.Outreach.com

All Scripture quotations are taken from THE HOLY BIBLE, NEW INTERNATIONAL VERSION®, NIV® Copyright © 1973, 1978, 1984, 2011 by Biblica, Inc.® Used by permission. All rights reserved worldwide.

ISBN: 9781942027317

Cover Design and Interior Design by Tim Downs

Written by Jeremy Jones

Edited by Tia Smith

Printed in the United States of America

CONTENTS

CHAPTER 1

AN INVITATION

The Christmas season is here. It's the most wonderful time of the year—or so the old song goes. Yet we all have to admit that it doesn't always feel that way. Each of us can rattle off a list of the reasons we feel a twinge of stress or sadness mixed with happiness or excitement when the carols start playing in every public setting. Hectic schedules, rampant materialism, and reminders of personal wounds are just a few of the reasons.

Whether you are the person who is ready to relax and savor the season because you did all your shopping and preparations months ago (not likely) or the person who dreads the busyness, responsibilities, or loneliness that steals your joy this time of year (much more likely), the Christmas season offers a unique opportunity to experience God's love and grace in the midst of real life. Christmas can still truly give us a taste of the most wonderful time in world history. Jesus—the Messiah, the Savior—came as the light into the darkness, stress, and pain of the world. That world then needed the light to illuminate, clarify, guide, and heal—just like our world now, including our lives, needs the very same thing. Christ's coming brings that ultimate light as well as His peace, joy, and all-consuming love. Those are the true gifts of Christmas. And He is worth celebrating.

Each of our celebrations will look a bit different depending on our places in life. You may be single, married, with or without or wishing for kids. You may be celebrating new life or grieving the loss of a loved one. You may be caring for older parents, young children, or someone who is sick. You may have every moment of your Christmas Eve and Christmas Day already scheduled, or you may be wondering how in the world you are going to fill all the holiday hours.

This invitation is for you, whoever you are and whatever your situation. Think about the people God invited to witness the birth of His Son that first Christmas—they came from all areas and walks of life.

First there were Mary and Joseph. They were young and in love, and God interrupted their lives with an invitation to follow Him. When the angel appeared to each of them, they were afraid. But they surrendered their own plans and followed God.

Luke 1 tells the story of how an angel appeared to Mary and explained that she would give birth to the Son of God. Although Mary was troubled and afraid, she responded in faith: "'I am the Lord's servant,' Mary answered. 'May your word to me be fulfilled.' Then the angel left her" (Luke 1:38).

Joseph's story is recorded in the book of Matthew. It tells us that Joseph found out his wife-to-be was pregnant. In other words, he had to endure the shock of bad news and feel the burden of his life plans unraveling. Then—afterward— Joseph was told by God what he should do. And when an angel explained God's plan to him, Joseph too responded in faith: "When Joseph woke up, he did what the angel of the Lord had commanded him and took Mary home as his wife. But he did not consummate their marriage until she gave birth to a son. And he gave him the name Jesus" (Matthew 1:24–25).

By trusting God, this young couple didn't sign up for honor, prestige, or excitement. Theirs was more a journey of rejection, doubt, and uncertainty. But they chose to follow each step of the way to Bethlehem and to be the vessels God used to bring His love and salvation to the world.

Then there were the shepherds. Talk about a motley crew. They were working on Christmas! But they had no choice. Shepherds were pretty low on the social scale in that day. Yet while they were tending to their sheep, their lives were interrupted by an angel announcing the birth of the Son of God. "An angel of the Lord appeared to them, and the glory of the Lord shone around them, and they were terrified. But the angel said to them, 'Do not be afraid. I bring you good news that will cause great joy for all the people. Today in the town of David a Savior has been born to you; he is the Messiah, the Lord'" (Luke 2:9–11).

The shepherds could have stayed in the field. They could have said they were busy. They could have assumed such an important message was meant for someone more worthy. They could have chosen not to go. But they eagerly left what they were doing and went to see what the angels had told them about. "When the angels had left them and gone into heaven, the shepherds said to one another, 'Let's go to Bethlehem and see this thing that has happened, which the Lord has told us about'" (Luke 2:15).

And then there were the Magi—you know, "we three kings of Orient are." The guys with gold, frankincense, and myrrh. They didn't quite make it to the manger scene in Bethlehem (although they usually show up in most Christmas pageants). But they did make the longest journey, following a star they believed signaled the birth of the Messiah. Matthew 2:1–2 tells us, "After Jesus was born in Bethlehem in Judea, during the time of King Herod, Magi from the east came to Jerusalem and asked, 'Where is the one who has been born king of the Jews? We saw his star when it rose and have come to worship him.'"

These wise men could have been skeptical or hoped someone else would go. They could have said the journey was too long or too hard. But they recognized the invitation of God to witness something that would change the world, and they went.

So what does your journey to Bethlehem look like? How has God been calling you to follow Him to Bethlehem and experience in a new way the birth of His Son, Jesus? Will you go? Will you set aside the distractions of life and allow God to lead you? Will you let the light of God's love shine into even the darkest places of your heart this Christmas season? Will you choose to experience Christmas as truly the most wonderful time of the year—not as an empty lyric but as a life-giving encounter? The invitation to you is the same as it was for Mary and Joseph, the shepherds, and the Magi—to come and see this baby born in a manger, Jesus, the Messiah, the Son of God, and to be changed by the experience.

This book is an invitation to do just that. It is not meant to provide you with more stuff to do. It's an invitation to fun, reflection, and community. It's an invitation for you to step into the glow of the light of the world, our Savior born as a baby in Bethlehem.

In the pages of this book, you will find a wide variety of ideas. You may already have holiday plans and traditions, or you may be looking for ideas to start some. Please know that this book is intended to be an inspiration, not a burden. Use it to supplement and add creativity. Take the ideas, activities, and devotions, and adapt them as you see fit to help you celebrate the miracle that is the birth of Jesus Christ.

If you've received this book early in the Christmas season, you'll find many ideas in the final chapter to use throughout the season. If you're just picking it up on Christmas Eve, you'll find a schedule to guide you and your family through a celebration of Christmas Eve and Christmas Day. In addition, there is a whole chapter on carrying the light of Christmas into the new year. So find your place, answer God's invitation, and let His love light your way as you journey to Bethlehem this Christmas.

CHAPTER 2

CELEBRATION SCHEDULE

Christmas Eve and Christmas Day are both times for celebration. In this chapter, you'll find a quick-reference outline of activities for these two special days. All the detailed instructions and resources are spelled out in chapters 3 and 4. So read through the descriptions in those chapters and then flip back to this schedule and make it your own. Get out your red—and green—pens. Add the things you already have planned. Star the parts you like. Cross out the ones you don't. If you need more or different ideas, check out chapter 7 of this book. Turn this schedule into one that works for you as you prepare to celebrate.

Christmas Eve

Afternoon

✦ *Read*: "Messenger of Light" in chapter 5 is an original Christmas fiction story to read and talk about together.

✦ *Serve*: Use the ideas provided to share the light of Christmas with others.

✦ *Connect*: Compose an e-mail newsletter to send to friends and family.

✦ *Create*: Make Mason jar star lanterns.

✦ *Recreate*: Stay healthy and burn some excess kid energy with a family hike, bike, or swim.

Evening

✦ *Worship*: Attend a Christmas Eve service.

✦ *Eat*: Do dinner differently by incorporating a new fun idea.

✦ *Read:* Prepare for Jesus's coming with the "Christmas Candles" devotion.

✦ *Celebrate:* Take a night walk and enjoy all the lights.

✦ *Play:* Open a Night Before Christmas box.

✦ *Relax:* Enjoy a quiet time of candlelight, music, and more.

Christmas Day

✦ *Give:* If giving and receiving presents is part of your tradition, fit them into your day of celebration when it works best for you.

Morning

✦ *Read:* Take time to read the Christmas story.

✦ *Eat:* Enjoy Christmas pancakes, cinnamon rolls, or your favorite holiday food.

✦ *Thank:* Form a "snowball circle" to share the things you're thankful for.

✦ *Play:* Organize a Christmas scavenger hunt.

Afternoon

✦ *Create:* Bake a birthday cake for Jesus, or make Christmas light paintings.

✦ *Serve*: Take a basket of dinner or holiday snacks to someone in need.

✦ *Play*: Enjoy a snow activity (or find a snow substitute if it's warm weather).

✦ *Connect*: Call, FaceTime, or send fun photos to family who can't be with you.

Evening

✦ *Read:* Read the "Darkness and Light" devotion.

✦ *Remember:* Start a holiday tradition by creating a Christmas Memory box.

CHAPTER 3

CHRISTMAS EVE

It's the night before Christmas! Follow this schedule for a fun and meaningful celebration. Whether you are reading, serving, connecting, playing, or relaxing, allow the suggestions here to help you open your heart to the light of Christmas as you anticipate the arrival of the Christ child.

Christmas Eve

Afternoon

✦ *Read*: "Messenger of Light," an original Christmas fiction story found in chapter 5, is great for kids and will touch the hearts of all ages. Find an uninterrupted time when everyone can sit together and listen to this story. Put the electronics away, light a candle or a fire, curl up with a blanket (or hang out in the hammock if your weather is warm), and read this Christmas story aloud. Then talk about it together. Questions provided at the end of the story can help prompt you and your family to think about how the message can change your hearts and lives this Christmas.

✦ *Serve*: There could be no greater blessing this Christmas Eve than sharing the light of Christmas with others. While many people are busy with family and last-minute Christmas preparations, others are alone and in need of God's love. If you are able to plan ahead, look for a local charity where you can help serve a meal. If Christmas Eve is upon you without a plan, take a plate of cookies and visit an elderly neighbor or a local retirement home. Many of the older people there will be far away from family and would love to have someone to simply sit and talk with on this holiday. Ask them to share their most memorable Christmas with you. Take an hour to set aside your own schedule, and open your heart and ears to listen to an older person. As you bless them, you are sure to be blessed.

+ *Connect:* Sure, the Christmas cards are all stamped and sent (or are they?). But your close family and friends would love a more detailed, real-life update of what you are up to this Christmas Eve. So recruit the youngest to the oldest and have them each write one short paragraph for a Christmas Eve e-mail. If they need inspiration, offer them sentence prompts to complete such as "My favorite thing about today has been . . ." or "If you were here, I'd love to . . ." Include some recent pictures, or have a fun photo session (ugly holiday sweaters, shaving cream elf beards, Santa hats and sunglasses, or your own creative idea) and send a shot or two with your e-mail. Whether your family and friends read it today or in the days following Christmas, it will help them feel more connected to those they love this season.

+ *Create:* Make these simple Mason jar star lanterns. Collect one small glass jar per person. Small jelly or canning jars work well—no lids needed. On the outside of the jars, have each person attach medium-sized star stickers or glue on paper star cutouts. Put a votive or tea light in the bottom of each jar. Use the jars as a centerpiece on the table or line them up on a bookshelf or mantle. Light the candles, and watch for the star shadows they cast on a nearby wall.

For a more involved project, place the star stickers on the jars, then spray-paint the outside of the jars red, green, gold, and silver. While the paint is still drying, remove the stickers. When you light a candle inside the jar, it will create a glowing star on a nearby wall instead of a star-shaped shadow.

✦ *Recreate*: By Christmas Eve, your family or group may already be feeling you've had too much time together under one roof—and maybe one too many cookies. Give your physical and mental health a boost by doing something active. Go for a family hike. Take a bike ride. Find an indoor pool and go for a swim. Take the family to a climbing gym or indoor trampoline park. Even when you love being with those you love, it's easy to let relational and logistical stress steal your ability to experience the wonder of Christmas. Make room for the wonder by releasing a little steam. The added benefit? Nothing like some good exercise to tire out the kids and help them sleep tonight when they are anticipating hearing reindeer hooves on the roof.

Evening

✦ *Worship*: Whether you are close to your home church or not, find a church and attend a Christmas Eve service. There is something wonderful about the body of Christ coming together to celebrate this night that changed the course of history. If you have kids, look for a service at an earlier time that caters to young hearts. If you are with an older crowd, consider a midnight service where you can worship together right at the start of Christmas Day.

✦ *Eat*: Do dinner differently! Use one of these fun ideas to create a Christmas Eve memory for all.

✦ Have a dress-up dinner complete with your best dishes, music, and candlelight. Make it a banquet fit for a king as you welcome the King of Kings to earth tonight.

✦ Pack the picnic basket and spread out a blanket right next to your Christmas tree for a picnic under the lights. This is a fun and easy dinner for young kids who will love the extra time looking at the tree and studying the presents they see.

✦ Have a make-your-own-pizza party. Give each
person a ball of dough and encourage creativity
to shape pizzas into holiday fun. Christmas trees,
wreaths, stars, and candy canes all make tasty
pizza shapes.

✦ *Read*: Prepare for Jesus's coming by using this "Christmas
Candles" devotion.

Devotion: Christmas Candles

"I can't wait for Christmas!" Those words are being said a
million times around the world tonight. Waiting can be ex-
citing, but it can also be hard. Patience is tough. But learn-
ing about the coming of Jesus and celebrating together can
make the waiting easier. In some Christian traditions, the
weeks leading up to Christmas are called Advent. They are
a time of waiting and expectation. Tonight we are going to
light five Christmas candles that represent different themes
of the Christmas story as we wait for Christmas. Sometimes
we view waiting as boring, but tonight's waiting is going to
be fun as we light the candles in anticipation of Jesus's birth.

We light candles because their light reminds us that Jesus is the light of the world. His light comes into the darkness of our lives to bring newness, life, and hope. It also reminds us that we are called to be a light to the world as people see the love of Jesus in us. Each time we light a candle, we remember part of the story of Jesus coming to earth as a baby, and we wait with excitement to celebrate what happens next.

Light each candle one at a time, and read the Bible passages listed. If your group is up for it, memorize the short focus verses together. Try making up hand motions to help kids and adults alike. Discuss what each candle signifies, and then sing the song together. To enhance the singing fun and keep everyone active, add some tambourines, maracas, or jingle bells to the singing.

Candle 1: Hope

Read: Isaiah 11:1–5 and Luke 1:26–38

Focus: Isaiah 9:6

Discuss: The first candle signifies the hope that people felt in their hearts for a Savior to lead them out of dark and hard times. What does it mean to hope for something? What had God promised to the people of Israel that they were hoping for? What do you hope for this Christmas?

Sing: "Away in a Manger"

Candle 2: Peace

Read: Luke 2:1–7

Focus: John 14:27a

Discuss: The second candle signifies peace and reminds us that Jesus came to bring peace and goodwill. What does it mean to have peace? Do you think it was peaceful in Bethlehem when Jesus was born? How can we have peace in our hearts when the world around us is not peaceful?

Sing: "Silent Night"

Candle 3: Joy

Read: Luke 2:8–14

Focus: Psalm 100:1

Discuss: The third candle represents joy and reminds us of the good news the angels brought to the shepherds. What do you think it was like when all those angels appeared in the dark night sky and sang together? How would you have felt if you were there? Why does Jesus's coming bring us joy?

Sing: "Joy to the World"

Candle 4: Love

Read: Luke 2:15–20

Focus: John 3:16

Discuss: The fourth candle represents love and reminds us that Jesus was sent to earth because of God's deep love for us. How did the shepherds spread God's love after they had gone to see Jesus? The wise men came later to see Jesus. How did they show their love for the new King? How can we show our love for Jesus?

Sing: "Hark the Herald Angels Sing"

Candle 5: Christ

You may choose to complete the lighting of the candles tonight, or save the final candle for Christmas morning. The Candle 5 information is included here and in the Christmas Day schedule in the next chapter.

Read: Luke 2:1–21

If appropriate, choose one of the children in the family to read the story, or have each family member read a few verses.

Focus: Reread (or recite together if you memorized them) the focus verses from the other four candles: Isaiah 9:6, John 14:27a, Psalm 100:1, and John 3:16.

Discuss: The fifth and final candle represents the gift God gave us in the baby Jesus, the Savior of the world. Why do we give gifts to each other on Christmas? What was the greatest gift of all? How can we share that gift with others today?

Sing: Choose a favorite or sing all the songs from the other four candles: "Away in a Manger," "Silent Night," "Joy to the World," and "Hark the Herald Angels Sing."

✦ Celebrate: When you are finished with the devotion time, take a night walk around the neighborhood to enjoy the festive lights of the season. As you walk, let the reality sink in that Jesus is the true light of the world.

✦ Play: Open a Night Before Christmas box. Place supplies for your Christmas Eve fun in a box, wrap it, and place it under the tree. Kids always want to open "just one present" on Christmas Eve, so after dinner, have them open the box and use the contents for an evening of fun together. You might include new pajamas, popcorn, and a new Christmas book, movie, board game, or puzzle for the family to enjoy together.

✦ *Relax:* Sometimes silence is the very best way to reflect on the season and prepare your heart for the coming of the Christ child. Whether you sit by the fire, light candles, turn on the Christmas lights, or sit in the dark, spend a few minutes in complete silence, letting God speak to your heart tonight. Even with young children, you can encourage a minute of silence—a time when everyone sits in quiet expectation of the coming of Jesus. Close your time of silence with a simple prayer, inviting Jesus into your world tonight, or by singing the well-known Christmas song "Silent Night."

Silent Night

Silent night, holy night

All is calm, all is bright

Round yon virgin, mother and child

Holy infant, so tender and mild

Sleep in heavenly peace

Sleep in heavenly peace

Silent night, holy night

Shepherds quake at the sight

Glories stream from heaven afar

Heavenly hosts sing alleluia

Christ the Savior is born

Christ the Savior is born

Silent night, holy night

Son of God, love's pure light

Radiant beams from Thy holy face

Jesus, Lord at Thy birth

Jesus, Lord at Thy birth

CHAPTER 4

CHRISTMAS DAY

Merry Christmas! The big day is finally here. After all the waiting and preparation, enjoy this day. May it be filled with joy and laughter, good friends and food, and a deep sense of the love of Emmanuel, God with us.

Christmas Day

✦ *Give:* If giving and receiving presents is part of your tradition, fit them into your day of celebration where it works best for you.

Morning

✦ *Read:* Begin your morning by lighting the final candle (see "Christmas Candles" devotion from Christmas Eve). Or if you chose to light all five candles on Christmas Eve, then reread the Christmas story, found in Luke 2:1–21, together.

Candle 5: Christ

Read: Luke 2:1–21

If appropriate, choose one of the children in the family to read the story, or have each family member read a few verses.

Focus: Reread (or recite together if you memorized them) the focus verses from last night's four candles: Isaiah 9:6, John 14:27a, Psalm 100:1, and John 3:16.

Discuss: The fifth and final candle represents the gift God gave us in the baby Jesus, the Savior of the world. Why do we give gifts to each other on Christmas? What was the greatest gift of all? How can we share that gift with others today?

Sing: Sing all the songs from last night's candles: "Away in a Manger," "Silent Night," "Joy to the World," and "Hark the Herald Angels Sing."

✦ *Eat:* Whether your tradition involves Christmas pancakes, cinnamon rolls, or another tasty breakfast menu, celebrate by eating together. If you don't have a family Christmas breakfast tradition, consider creating one this year and make it part of your celebration for years to come.

✦ *Thank*: Set aside a few minutes when you can all spend time giving thanks. This may work well before you open gifts or just after a meal together. Make it fun by forming a "snowball circle" to encourage everyone to share the things they are thankful for. Have everyone stand or sit in a circle. Use a real snowball, an ice cube, or a cotton ball as the snowball. Throw the "ball" to someone in the group, who shares something they are thankful for on this Christmas Day. When they are finished, they quickly throw the snowball to someone else. When everyone has had a chance to share, say a prayer of thanksgiving, acknowledging that God is the giver of all good gifts.

✦ *Play*: Create a Christmas scavenger hunt. Divide family members into teams and give each team a list of the items they are to find and a Christmas gift bag to collect them in. The first team back to the kitchen with all the items in the bag wins candy canes! Use the list below or create one of your own.

   ✦ One empty stocking

   ✦ An ornament hook

   ✦ Three needles from the Christmas tree

   ✦ A Christmas card with a dog in the picture

- One piece of chocolate

- A candle

- One Christmas ribbon

- Six cranberries

- A Christmas DVD case

- A piece of colored tissue paper

- One holiday-themed book

- And a partridge in a pear tree (get creative here ... maybe draw it, create it with clay or Legos, or find a picture in a book)

Afternoon

- *Create:* It's Jesus's birthday! So gather the troops and work together to make a birthday cake for Jesus. If the kitchen is busy with holiday meal preparations, you might opt for an art project instead. Gather some white paper, washable paints, wet rags, and markers. Have everyone dip a thumb in the paint and make a thumbprint on the paper to look like a colorful Christmas lightbulb. Once there are lots of colorful thumbprints, use the markers to draw a curling line to connect the thumbprints into a string of Christmas lights. Hang the painting in a window where the sunlight can shine through the colored thumbprints to make the lights look like they are shining.

✦ *Serve:* Take some time today to serve others. It can be official, like delivering a basket of dinner to someone in need. Or it can be spontaneous, like getting out to shovel the snow off the sidewalk for your neighbors. It may involve driving someone without transportation to a holiday gathering. Or perhaps simply calling a friend you need to connect with again. It may mean volunteering to do the dishes or watching the kids so the parents can get out for a short walk. Whatever you do, make a conscious effort to serve someone and spread some Christmas cheer today.

✦ *Play:* If you've got Christmas snow, get out in it! Go sledding, build a snowman, or have a snowball fight. If there's no snow or you find yourself in a warm climate, create some snow-substitute activities. Sled down a grass or sand hill, and have a marshmallow snowball fight. The long-lasting memories will be the ones you create sharing fun and laughter together.

✦ *Connect*: Use technology to bring those who are far away into your celebration today. Whether you call, FaceTime, text, or post photos, take the time to connect with friends and family who are far away.

Evening

✦ *Read*: Celebrate the coming of Jesus with this "Darkness and Light" devotion.

Devotion: Darkness and Light

Gather your family in the darkest room in your house. Try to get everyone in a room or closet that is absolutely pitch dark. Now hand out paper and pencils and tell everyone to try drawing a picture of the nativity scene. Once that is done, give everyone a handful of Skittles and ask them to separate the candy into piles by color. In the dark, these things are impossible! Now light one small candle or turn on a small flashlight. Try the activities again and talk about how even a small amount of light transforms the darkness. Then read the following together.

What does light do? First, light gets our attention. Think about lightning in a thunderstorm. When light flashes across a dark sky, it catches our eye and we know thunder isn't far behind. That first Christmas, angels lit up the sky to announce the birth of Jesus to some shepherds out in a field. The light and the message that followed got the attention of the shepherds and sent them on their way to witness God's Son sent to earth.

Light also shows us the way. Think of the wise men in the Christmas story. How did they know where to go to find Jesus? They followed the light—a star that led them to Bethlehem. Jesus is still the light of the world today. As we've talked about, Jesus gets our attention and then shows us the way to live.

In Genesis 1:3–5, "God said, 'Let there be light,' and there was light. God saw that the light was good, and he separated the light from the darkness. God called the light 'day,' and the darkness he called 'night.' And there was evening, and there was morning—the first day."

From the beginning of Creation, God has been the creator and giver of light. Genesis tells us He made light in the darkness at Creation. Then thousands of years later, He sent His light to earth in Jesus.

"For God, who said, 'Let light shine out of darkness,' made his light shine in our hearts to give us the light of the knowledge of God's glory displayed in the face of Christ" (2 Corinthians 4:6).

So what should our response be?

> This is the message we have heard from him and declare to you: God is light; in him there is no darkness at all. If we claim to have fellowship with him and yet walk in the darkness, we lie and do not live out the truth. But if we walk in the light, as he is in the light, we have fellowship with one another, and the blood of Jesus, his Son, purifies us from all sin. (1 John 1:5–7)

God's purpose for sending His Son to earth was so that through Jesus's death on the cross and resurrection, each one of us could be forgiven of our sins and walk with God in the light of His love. How should that change the way we celebrate today?

✦ *Remember:* Start a tradition by creating a Christmas Memory box. Decorate a shoe box or photo box (great activity for kids or teens) and include your family name on the top. This can be as simple or elaborate as you like. Then give each person present at today's Christmas celebration a piece of paper. Encourage everyone to think of one thing they'd like to remember about this Christmas, and write it down or draw a picture of it on the paper. Ask them to include their name and the year on the back of the paper. Once everyone has finished, place the papers in the box and put it somewhere for safekeeping until next year. Each Christmas night for years to come, you can add to the memories and pull out the papers from previous years to read fun reminders of the many things you did and shared on Christmases past.

CHAPTER 5

MESSENGER
OF LIGHT

Heavy wet snowflakes fell silently and clung to the snowy owl's downy white feathers. He shook the snowy coat from his head as he raised his wings and glided low and silently across the land. The darkness of the night quickly enveloped him as dense clouds and fog blocked out even the hint of light from the moon or stars. This Christmas Eve was the darkest of nights.

But on the edge of the snowy horizon, a soft yellow glow emerged within the darkness—the light of a fire shone from a small cabin tucked into a low hillside and half buried in drifts of snow. Inside, a mother and father sat sipping warm cider from their mugs while their son and daughter played cards beside the hearth. There was nothing impressive about the little cabin. The main room held nothing more than a rough-hewn table and bench, two chairs, a stove, and a small round rug covering the planks beside the fireplace. One chair was pulled close to the fireplace so the son could prop his leg up on the hearth. A bandage wrapped from his knee to his ankle disguised a leg misshapen from a terrible fall. But you would never guess at his pain tonight—only laughter and singing filled the tiny home this Christmas Eve.

Outside the cabin, a narrow snow-packed trail snaked across an alpine tundra meadow before plunging down a steep ravine and eventually to a town in the valley below. It was at the edge of that steep ravine, along a knife-edge cliff, that a man bundled against the cold cautiously placed one foot in front of the other. He shivered and pulled his scarf tighter around his neck and mouth. He turned his head aside as the wind blasted his cheeks.

I should never have come out here tonight, he thought to himself. *Why didn't I stay home by the fire?* But the question only echoed against the gnawing shadows within. He knew why. The loneliness of his big, empty house on this holiday night had been too much to bear. Restless and unable to relax, he'd needed to get out and clear his mind, breathe in the cold fresh air. But after hiking farther than usual, the fog was making it impossible for him to get his bearings. The heavy snowfall covered his tracks. Fear seized him as he realized he was lost. Alone. In a snowstorm. On Christmas Eve. His foot slipped, and he stumbled to the ground. *I'll just rest here for a minute*, he thought. But a minute turned to a few minutes, which turned to an hour. Heaviness seeped into his bones. Tired and nearly frozen, he couldn't muster the strength to get up.

Overhead, the snowy owl's sharp night vision caught sight of the slightest movement on the ground below. In silence, he swooped close in hopes of finding dinner. Instead, the owl found the end of a red scarf whipping in the wind. Attracted by the motion, he circled back, grabbed an end, and flew upward. There was only a gentle tug of resistance, and the scarf came loose easily. Holding it tight in his talons, the owl flew back toward his home. With a perfect sense of direction, he flew through the storm and soon saw the only light for miles, glowing from a single cabin window. Gracefully he lighted on the windowsill. With the scarf still in his talons, he stood stone still on the sill and stared into the cheerful room.

Inside, the family exchanged simple gifts. The son received a new pair of warm wool socks. The daughter's hands made a muffled sound as she clapped them together inside a new pair of cozy mittens.

"Oh, thank you!" they both said, giving hugs to their mother and father.

Holding his wife's hand, Father replied with a smile, "I just wish we had more to give. But I'm so thankful for the gift of family and of time to celebrate the birth of Christ together."

"What more could we need?" the mother replied. She followed her husband's eyes, which were fixed intently on their son's bandaged leg. She knew her husband would give anything to have the money to get his son the proper medical care he needed. He couldn't bear the thought of this injury limiting his son for life.

"I'm sure it will heal, Dad," said the son, also noticing his father's gaze. "Just takes a little time and patience." He smiled, but no one missed the fact that he winced in pain as he lowered his foot from the hearth to the floor.

What they *did* miss was the owl. The observant bird had not moved from the windowsill. There he stood, still as a statue, with his gaze fixed inside the cabin. It wasn't until Mother walked to the stove to refill her mug that she caught sight of those haunting yellow eyes and jumped.

"Aaahhh!" she cried. "Look! The owl—I'm sure it's the one from our meadow. What on earth is it doing?"

The whole family turned to look. Only then did the owl spread its powerful wings wide. In one quick motion, it lifted the scarf up to its beak.

"What in the world?" mumbled Father. "What does he have?"

"Looks like some old bandanna," guessed Sister, shrugging. "A hiker probably dropped it in the forest last fall."

Father gently and cautiously lifted the window. The owl did not fly away but jumped to the side, leaving the scarf on the sill when Father reached out a hand.

"This is no rag from the forest," said Father softly, winding the scarf around his hand. "It's a wool scarf—a fine and expensive wool scarf."

"Do you think someone lost it?" asked Mother.

Father looked from the scarf to the owl, who was still staring.

"I don't think the scarf is lost," said Father slowly. "I think a person is lost."

"Tonight?" Mother exclaimed. "On Christmas Eve? In this kind of weather? Who would go out?"

"I'm not sure," said Father, starting to pull on his boots. "But I have to go look. If for no other reason, to get that crazy owl to stop staring at me from the windowsill."

Mother pressed a firm hand against her son's shoulder as he started to get up from his seat. "You're not really going to let a red scarf and a wild staring owl send you out in this storm, are you?" she asked Father.

"The last time that owl had that look in his eye was when our son needed help," he replied. "I have to go."

"But that's crazy," argued Mother. "You don't really think the owl knows . . ."

"He's right, Mom," said Brother softly. "If it's nothing, Dad will be back soon. If someone is out there in this cold, they won't make it to see the light of morning."

With that, it was settled. The whole family scurried about helping Father gather his warmest gear, as well as a blanket and some warm cider in case he found someone in need of help. Father wrapped a rag around the end of a long stick, soaked it in kerosene, and placed it in the fire until it was a blazing torch. Then he turned to go.

"Be safe," said Mother as she held the door open against the blast of wintery air. When the door slammed shut, the owl lifted silently into the air.

Father trudged through the deep snow. His bright torch only lit the way a few feet in front of him. Each time he thought of turning back, he looked and could make out the tail feathers of the owl flying low just ahead. So he pressed on. Just when he was ready to give up, the shadow of a mound close to the ridge in front of him caught his eye. He hurried ahead and found the man who had lost his way huddled in a ball and nearly covered with snow. The man was almost frozen, but he lifted his head when Father came close. Father threw the blanket over the man and held the thermos of warm cider to his lips. Then, lifting him up, Father practically carried the man back through the snow to the cabin.

An hour later, bundled by the fire, full of warm food and drink, the man thanked his rescuer. But never wanting the attention on himself, Father quickly asked his kids to start up the Christmas carols where they had left off. The children began to sing while their guest kept the beat by tapping his mug against the arm of his chair. It was a jubilant

Christmas Eve with a stranger for company and Father safely back in the cabin. Their guest didn't say much, but as the night wore on, the man slowly regained strength, and the family gladly shared the warmth and light of their Christmas Eve with him.

The next morning dawned bright and clear. The dark fog of the night before had given way to golden sun that glistened on the snowy white crystals all around.

Mother and Father came quietly into the cabin's main room to try to stoke the fire without disturbing anyone. But they quickly realized that their guest was no longer here; he was gone. They did find a simple note placed on top of the red scarf at the center of the old wooden table. Scrawled across a scrap of paper, the note read:

Thank you, my friends. A million times, thank you. You saved my life in more ways than you know. Not only was I nearly frozen in the storm, my heart was stone cold. For the past two years since my wife's death, I have been living a lonely and selfish life. The light of your Christmas fire and the love of your family reminded me of the many reasons I have to live and the many things I have to give others. I'd love to stay to celebrate Christmas Day, but I must go visit friends and family and begin to make things right. My office is in the town center. I expect to see your son there as soon as you can make it safely down the mountain. No appointment needed. No payment accepted.

Blessings this Christmas Day!

Dr. Hanslow

Father's eyes were glassy with tears as he sunk into a chair and handed the note to Mother. Warm salt water rushed to her eyes as she looked from the note to Father in amazement.

"The doctor," she said softly, holding the note to her heart. "You saved the doctor."

Father heard the children stirring in their beds and stood up quickly. "Merry Christmas!" he hollered loudly to them as he pulled on his gloves and walked outside to gather logs from the woodpile stacked against the side of the cabin. He filled his lungs with a long, deep breath of the clean, frigid air and looked up to the sky. There, silhouetted against the bright blue, was the snowy owl. "Whooo whooo!" came the distinctive cry of the owl as he flew overhead.

"Crazy owl. What do you want now?" said Father with a chuckle. "Oh, you've come to wish me a Merry Christmas? Ha! No one would believe me if I told them about you." He shook his head and looked away.

"Whooo whooo!" answered the owl, louder this time as it circled and landed on a nearby fence post.

"Really?" asked Father with a grin as he looked intently

into the bright yellow eyes. "Who, you ask? Don't you know whose birthday it is? Today we celebrate Jesus, the Son of God, the light of the world."

Father turned his back to the owl and laughed out loud. The snowy owl opened his full, broad wingspan and rose from the fence into the air as Father nudged the cabin door open and stepped inside to join his family by the warmth and light of the Christmas fire.

Discuss

Talk together about some or all of the following questions:

✦ What is your favorite part of the story?

✦ Would you have followed the owl into the snowy night? Why or why not?

✦ Who in the story received the most help?

✦ Whom do we know who may be hurting? How can we offer them love and encouragement?

✦ How does light overcome darkness in this story?

✦ How has light overcome darkness in our world and lives?

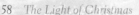

CHAPTER 6

CARRY THE LIGHT

It's not until the gifts are unwrapped, the meals are eaten, and the excitement dies down that Christmas really begins. Will the light of Christmas get packed away with the ornaments, or will it live and grow inside of us each day of the coming year? The baby born in Bethlehem grows up, teaches His disciples, and commits the ultimate act of love by dying on a cross for the sin of the world.

So let the celebration continue! You may still have kids out of school, family staying in your home, and vacation days left to use, so here is a devotion to share together and some great ideas to help you carry the light of Christmas into the new year.

Devotion: Carry the Light

Months before every winter and summer Olympic Games, the Olympic torch travels great distances through a torch relay, getting people's attention, inspiring them, and inviting them to the start of the games. The torch relay keeps the spirit of the games alive. As it travels, the light of the torch invites people to notice and watch and join. When it arrives at the final destination, a larger Olympic torch is lit to officially kick off the beginning of a new Olympic Games.

And while the Olympic tradition goes back to ancient Greece, the torch relay was started much more recently at the 1936 Olympic Games. The first Olympic torch relay carried a message the world did not need to hear. It wasn't a message of light, but of darkness. Hitler and his regime used the torch relay to promote and attract people to the Nazi movement.

Since that time, the torch relay has been used to purposefully promote good in the world. Each Olympic host city chooses a theme—a message they want to spread to the world. The 1948 London Games relay spread a message of peace as it traveled throughout Europe, which had been devastated by World War II. The 2000 Sydney Games connected Australia and its historical culture to the great island region of Oceania.

There is not just one way to carry the light of the torch—it has been carried by people on foot, dogsled, camelback, skis, snowboard, train, plane, boat, ice skates, wheelchair, and more. It has traveled to every corner of the globe through mountains, valleys, rivers, oceans, ice, under water, and even to outer space.

Jesus's coming to earth was the start of a different sort of torch relay. It is an opportunity for each person who believes in Him to carry His message of love and salvation to the world. Why do we still need to carry the message that was started so long ago? John 1:4–5 says, "In him was life, and that life was the light of all mankind. The light shines in the darkness, and the darkness has not overcome it."

Jesus did not rid the earth of all darkness when He came, but His light shines in the darkness and the people around us still need His light. As those who live in God's light, we have the opportunity to spread the light—the message of God's love.

Organize your own family torch relay using a candle or flashlight. Have each person choose the message they want to carry and communicate to the world. As the first person lights their torch or turns on their flashlight, have them say their message out loud, then make a loop around the course you've set. When they return, they can hand the light off to the next family member to say their message out loud and complete their part of the torch relay.

When everyone is finished, read Matthew 5:16. "In the same way, let your light shine before others, that they may see your good deeds and glorify your Father in heaven."

How can each of us carry the light of Christmas in our lives every day? The angels and shepherds and wise men didn't leave the light of Christmas in a stable in Bethlehem; they left and told everyone they saw about what they had experienced. In the same way we can share the message of Christmas with those we meet by telling them about our own experiences and asking about theirs. And however we share it, the core of our message should always be the message Jesus taught: "I am the light of the world. Whoever follows me will never walk in darkness, but will have the light of life" (John 8:12).

Close with a prayer for courage and steadfastness to carry the light of Jesus into the world.

More Ideas to Carry the Light After Christmas

✦ Make a Christmas box ornament and fill it with fun memories from the past year. Hang it on the tree and open it on New Year's Eve as you reflect on the past year and look forward to a new year.

✦ Now that the presents are opened and there is more room under the tree, have a slumber party by the tree. Pull out the sleeping bags and watch old movies of your family or a holiday movie you missed during the season.

✦ Create a prayer basket. Place all the Christmas cards you received in a basket on your dining table. Each day choose one Christmas card and pray for the friends or family who sent that card. Sometime during the day, send that person or family a text or e-mail and let them know you are thinking of and praying for them today.

✦ Write those thank-you notes! Make a list on a whiteboard of people who need to be thanked and what they gave. Then pop some popcorn, crank up the music, and have everyone start writing. As each thank-you note is completed, erase the name from the board until the whiteboard is white again.

✦ Compile the photos of the season into a printed photo book or online slide show to send to loved ones who couldn't be present this Christmas.

✦ Reconnect with a friend you haven't seen in a long time. Meet for lunch or a cup of coffee.

✦ Make a Keep Christmas Alive calendar. Plan one activity per month to help you carry the light of Christmas with you throughout the year. A sample calendar could look like this:

   ✦ January: Go back and see the elderly person you met while visiting the nursing home on Christmas Eve.

   ✦ February: This month can be lonely now that all the holiday festivities are over and the decorations are packed away. Invite your neighbors over for an open house or game night.

   ✦ March: Place a candle and an encouraging note in a gift bag and hang on a friend's doorknob.

   ✦ April: Read 1 John 1:5–7: "This is the message

we have heard from him and declare to you: God is light; in him there is no darkness at all. If we claim to have fellowship with him and yet walk in the darkness, we lie and do not live out the truth. But if we walk in the light, as he is in the light, we have fellowship with one another, and the blood of Jesus, his Son, purifies us from all sin." Print this verse on a card or write it on your mirror to help you memorize it.

✦ May: Use black paper and white chalk to create your own drawing or representation of light.

✦ June: Take a night hike. Use flashlights and sing Christmas carols as you hike.

✦ July: Have a Christmas in July day. Buy a simple gift for each family member and bake cookies together to deliver to a local fire department.

✦ August: Sleep under the stars—in your backyard, on the beach, or on the side of a mountain. Get away from the lights of the city where you can truly see the stars.

✦ September: Go back and read the Christmas

fiction story from chapter 5. Does it have any new meaning to you outside of the holiday season?

✦ October: Turn out the lights and crank up the music and create a family flashlight laser show on the walls.

✦ November: Look at home movies or pictures from last Christmas to kick off a new holiday season.

✦ December: Create a playlist of Christmas songs about light.

✦ After all the activity of the holidays, take some time to reflect on God's goodness. Find a quiet place and write or draw the things you are thankful for this season. Look for a place in nature to help inspire your thoughts—a favorite rock or tree to sit by. Or if the weather outside is frightful, light a fire or take a warm bubble bath. Relax and let your heart and mind give thanks. "Arise, shine, for your light has come, and the glory of the Lord rises upon you" (Isaiah 60:1).

CHAPTER 7

'TIS THE SEASON

While this book has spelled out some great ways to spend Christmas Eve and Christmas Day, there is truly a whole season to celebrate. Pick and choose from these great activities to get your heart and the hearts of those around you ready to welcome Jesus. It's a busy season, so some of these ideas can be done on the go as you run from one activity to another. Others are intended to help you slow down, take a break from the busyness, and focus on the true meaning of Christmas. Still others give you the chance to let the light of Christmas shine more brightly in the lives of those around you. Choose the ones that fit your life best, and enjoy the season!

Snow Cones: Collect some real (clean) snow from outside. Pack it into bowls, add juice, and enjoy.

Stocking Notes: Write the name of each family member on a slip of paper, and put the names in a cup or hat. Have each person draw the name of someone else in the family. Then have everyone take time to write their person an encouraging note (or draw a picture for them) and put it in their stocking on Christmas Eve.

Live Nativity: Visit a live nativity in your community, or create your own!

Non-White Elephant Gifts: For a more fun version of a white elephant gift exchange, add some action. On the top of each gift, place a sticky note with an instruction on it. When the person chooses and opens the gift, they also have to perform the action on the note. For example, you might write down things like "Sing the first verse of 'Rudolph, the Red-Nosed Reindeer,'" "Trade presents with a person wearing green," or "Walk around the circle balancing your gift on your head." Prepare to laugh!

Christmas Trivia: Create a Christmas trivia game by writing some questions on note cards. The questions can be about the first Christmas like: "What animals are mentioned in the Christmas story?" or "Who told the shepherds about Jesus's birth?" For a challenge, try: "Who was governor of Syria when the census took place?" Or they can be family tradition questions like: "Where did you spend your favorite Christmas?" or "What is the funniest gift you've ever received?" Keep the cards in your purse or backpack for some on-the-go Christmas fun.

Christmas Caroling: Share the joy of Christmas with friends in your neighborhood by going door-to-door singing Christmas songs. If anyone plays an instrument, have them bring it along. Even drums for the young ones and kazoos for the teens make a festive Christmas caroling band.

Advent Weeks: Use the Christmas Eve "Christmas Candles" devotion and spread it out over the season. Light one candle each Sunday before Christmas and then conclude with lighting the final candle on Christmas Eve.

Salt-Dough Nativity: Make some salt dough and mold pieces into the shapes of Mary, Joseph, Baby Jesus, the stable, animals, etc. Once it has dried, choose a place to display your new nativity scene.

Pay It Forward: When you find yourself out in the hustle and bustle of the Christmas season, make it a point to spread some cheer. Pay for the coffee of the person behind you in the drive-thru, let the person in line behind you at the grocery store go ahead of you, put a dollar in every bell ringer's bucket you see. Look for ways to show extravagant generosity this season.

Light Science: Do an Internet search for science experiments about light, and perform some with your kids. You'll have fun and learn something along the way.

Christmas Around the World: Create new family traditions by looking up the many ways people in other parts of the world celebrate Christmas. Try a new activity, recipe, or story, and experience the richness of the fact that God's love shown through Jesus is for the whole world.

Car Cards: Gather some card-making supplies (paper, stickers, markers, etc.) and put them in a box in the car. While you are running errands around town, or traveling to a holiday gathering, the kids can entertain themselves and help spread some Christmas cheer. Send the cards to friends, drop them in neighbors' mailboxes, or deliver them to a local police or fire station.

Compose a Carol: Rewrite the words to your favorite Christmas carol or holiday song. Make up a verse or rewrite the whole song. Older kids will have fun filming music videos for their new Christmas hits.

Babysitting Services: Provide babysitting for a busy mom or couple so they can get Christmas preparations done.

Christmas Poem: Read the classic poem below by Henry Wadsworth Longfellow, first published in 1858. While it doesn't follow the biblical account of the wise men exactly, it artistically represents the perspective of one group of people who came to welcome Jesus into the world. Talk through some questions about the poem: How does this poem help you identify with the wise men? What do you see in a new way after reading their story in this format? Are there any similarities you can find between their journey to Bethlehem and your journey to experience Jesus this Christmas season?

The Three Kings

Three Kings came riding from far away,

    Melchior and Gaspar and Baltasar;

Three Wise Men out of the East were they,

And they travelled by night and they slept by day,

    For their guide was a beautiful, wonderful star.

The star was so beautiful, large, and clear,

    That all the other stars of the sky

Became a white mist in the atmosphere,

And by this they knew that the coming was near

    Of the Prince foretold in the prophecy.

Three caskets they bore on their saddle-bows,

    Three caskets of gold with golden keys;

Their robes were of crimson silk with rows

Of bells and pomegranates and furbelows,

    Their turbans like blossoming almond-trees.

And so the Three Kings rode into the West,

    Through the dusk of night, over hill and dell,

And sometimes they nodded with beard on breast

And sometimes talked, as they paused to rest,

    With the people they met at some wayside well.

"Of the child that is born," said Baltasar,

    "Good people, I pray you, tell us the news;

For we in the East have seen his star,

And have ridden fast, and have ridden far,

    To find and worship the King of the Jews."

And the people answered, "You ask in vain;

    We know of no King but Herod the Great!"

They thought the Wise Men were men insane,

As they spurred their horses across the plain,

    Like riders in haste, who cannot wait.

And when they came to Jerusalem,

    Herod the Great, who had heard this thing,

Sent for the Wise Men and questioned them;

And said, "Go down unto Bethlehem,

And bring me tidings of this new king."

So they rode away; and the star stood still,

The only one in the grey of morn;

Yes, it stopped—it stood still of its own free will,

Right over Bethlehem on the hill,

The city of David, where Christ was born.

And the Three Kings rode through the gate and the guard,

Through the silent street, till their horses turned

And neighed as they entered the great inn-yard;

But the windows were closed, and the doors were barred,

And only a light in the stable burned.

And cradled there in the scented hay,

In the air made sweet by the breath of kine,

The little child in the manger lay,

The child, that would be king one day

    Of a kingdom not human but divine.

His mother Mary of Nazareth

    Sat watching beside his place of rest,

Watching the even flow of his breath,

For the joy of life and the terror of death

    Were mingled together in her breast.

They laid their offerings at his feet:

    The gold was their tribute to a King,

The frankincense, with its odor sweet,

Was for the Priest, the Paraclete,

    The myrrh for the body's burying.

And the mother wondered and bowed her head,

    And sat as still as a statue of stone;

Her heart was troubled yet comforted,

Remembering what the Angel had said

    Of an endless reign and of David's throne.

Then the Kings rode out of the city gate,

    With a clatter of hoofs in proud array;

But they went not back to Herod the Great,

For they knew his malice and feared his hate,

    And returned to their homes by another way.